South London Verses

Edited By Connor Matthews

First published in Great Britain in 2018 by:

 Young**Writers**

Young Writers
Remus House
Coltsfoot Drive
Peterborough
PE2 9BF
Telephone: 01733 890066
Website: www.youngwriters.co.uk

FOREWORD

Young Writers was established in 1991, dedicated to encouraging reading and creative writing in young people. Our nationwide writing initiatives are designed to inspire ideas and give pupils the incentive to write, and in turn develop literacy skills and confidence, whilst participating in a fun, imaginative activity.

Few things are more encouraging for the aspiring writer than seeing their own work in print, so we are proud that our anthologies are able to give young authors this unique sense of confidence and pride in their abilities.

For our latest competition, Rhymecraft, primary school pupils were asked to enter a land of poetry where they used poetic techniques such as rhyme, simile and alliteration to bring their ideas to life. The result is an entertaining and imaginative anthology which will make a charming keepsake for years to come.

Each poem showcases the creativity and talent of these budding new writers as they learn the skills of writing, and we hope you are as entertained by them as we are.

CONTENTS

Durand Academy, Lambeth

Aileen Ordonez-Castro (11)	48
Cheyanne Meghie (11)	50
Chenai Jordan (8)	52
Elena Agostinelli (11)	54
Bethanie Adeyeye (10)	55
Prisca Conteh (9)	56
Mert Alp Aydin (11)	57
Fares Amir Ouanoufi (10)	58
Racheal Olaleye (10)	59
Daniel Samuels (8)	60
Abigail Daniel Gebresillassie (9)	61
Alexia Tianna Clarke (9)	62
Joshua Augustin (11)	63
Shyla Dana Fenton-Duhaney (9)	64
Kendra Mauricio Santana (9)	65
Andre (9) & Kai Watson	66
Dominion Balogun (9)	67
Rianne Mercurius (9)	68
Izaiah Hudson (9)	69
Christabel Amoah (8)	70
Ahmed Hagos (8)	71
Boushra Hagos (10)	72
Ilyaas Gouten (9)	73
Wonuola Amole (9)	74
Samira Tahir Abdu (9)	75
Shanhi Paris Adelise (9)	76
Jesse Kobina Afful (8)	77
Shakina Mensah (9)	78
Harley Taylor (11)	79
Iqrah Sharifjama (10)	80
Zerina Turay (10)	81
Myah Lorraine Lewis-Whitley (8)	82
Fatima Mahfoodh (8)	83
Tizara Diamond Josephs (8)	84
Idriis Mohamed (8)	85
Daniel Caldeira Coelho (10)	86
Tristine Wanjiku Kamau (9)	87
Kaysha Bailey (8)	88
Azario Maigwa (9)	89
Nobel Frezghi (9)	90
Joshua Frezghi (10)	91
Nevaeh Boateng (11)	92

Deborah Daramola (9)	93
Saron Robel (10)	94
Darryl Asante-Yeboah (11)	95
Fatym Karmoko (9)	96
Kai Mills (9)	97
Nathaniel France (8)	98
Kareece Stephens (8)	99
Cameron Smith (8)	100
Micah Licorish (8)	101
Emily Mullen (8)	102

Holy Cross RC Primary School, Fulham

Rewan Josef (10)	103
Shalom Michreteab (9)	104

Hotham Primary School, Putney

Ella Tsang (9)	105
Sofia Peon (8)	106
Ava Grace McAndie (9)	108
Gemma McLean (8)	110
Samuel Augusto (9)	112
Matey Grantcharov (9)	113
Melody Fitzpatrick (9)	114
Musa Ahmed (9)	115
Neva Jansen (9)	116
Erika Grace Hashimoto (9)	117
Annebelle Kruger (8)	118
Gregory Daniel Hughes (8)	119
Alanna Garcia (8)	120
Nnenna Anna Naeche (9)	121
Celo Gilchrist (9)	122
Zack River Greenhough (9)	123
Bruno Carvalho de Andrade (9)	124
Zoë Sellers (8)	125
Haydn Wilkes (9)	126
Ava Jane Mason (8)	127
Sophie Killick (9)	128
Zoser McCalla (9)	129
William Saich (8)	130
Lina Yoshida (8)	131

Jessop Primary School, Herne Hill

Shumayl Ahmed	132
Sufyan Ahmed	133

Jubilee Primary School, Tulse Hill

Sadaq Asad Ahmed (11)	134

St George's Cathedral Catholic Primary School, Southwark

Chikamso Ukor-George (10)	135
Rowlanda Ken-Williams (11)	136
Jose Gabriel Abanto (11)	137
Zarin Anjum Ahmed (9)	138
Nathaniel Louis Bernardo Bardos (9)	139
Mica-Renee Quiazon (11)	140
Ivie Channell Ekhibise (10)	141
Andrea Miles Stallion-Orbista (11)	142
Rebecca Tenagne Kassa (9)	143
Daryl Gaid (8)	144
Alicia Oyedele (11)	145
Vernice Cuevas (8)	146
Julianna Ysabelle Valenzona (11)	147

St John The Divine CE Primary School, Camberwell

Nathaniel Marfo (10)	148
Camilla Kai Mensah (10)	149
David Alejandro Hannam Valles (9)	150
Inayaht Hussain	151
Andrea Carrera (9)	152
Rihann Mitchell	153
Maya Abdelwasi	154

The Chelsea Group Of Children, Wandsworth

Lara Talbot (10)	155
Gabi Reder (10)	156

THE POEMS

The Ocean Poem

The wind billows in the sail
Crewmen work hard and long
The mice squeal, small and frail
They all live on the boat lifelong.

Crewmen work hard and long
They wander across a watery trail
They all live on the boat lifelong
And on the sea, the boat does sail.

They wander across a watery trail
And all the men go along
And on the sea, the boat does sail
Yet all the men they still stay strong.

They all live on the boat lifelong
And water is tossed out with a pail -
Yet all the men they still stay strong
They live on through the gale.

Athena Horn (10)

Candy Land

Skittles and Smarties and chocolate rivers too,
Cows that make candy canes say moo.
All around me there were pure ice cream houses,
All with the cherries on top.
Then as I ambled over to the ice cream houses
I was stopped by some guards
Made of chocolate ice cream.
Me being me I just ignored what they said
And devoured them in a flash.
Then I knew it was a spell
Because the spell was wearing off.
I finally was in my home safe and sound,
But very sad and miserable.

Dorcas Ibukunoluwa Jaiyeola (9)

Creepy-Crawlies

Creepy-crawlies spinning around,
Some in the air, some on the ground.
Creepy-crawlies wriggling free,
They're what we call minibeasts.
Worms dig holes covered in slime,
Snails and slugs slip and slide.
They munch and crunch like caterpillars.
They'll eat all your veg for their dinner.
Creepy-crawlies moving like bees,
They fly in the air when they need to wee.
Creepy-crawlies like to eat,
They like to eat things like meat.
Creepy-crawlies are really weak,
They are the world's minibeasts.
Creepy-crawlies are all around,
They are in the air and underground.
Creepy-crawlies all around,
We need them to hear the sound.
Creepy-crawlies are neat,
They like to be neat with wheat.

Fahreed Oluwafikayomi Balogun (8)
Archbishop Sumner Primary School, Lambeth

Flower Power Land

In the land of the robot insects
A royal busy bee was king,
He'd be seen all day,
Buzzing away,
Wearing a crown while he'd whistle and sing.

Now the thing that made him happy,
Was the nectar that would give him power,
He'd fly up the hill,
Past Jack and Jill
And land on a tall sunflower.

One summer's day, so hot and dry,
Not a cloud to be seen in the sky,
The flower turned brown,
And it wilted to the ground,
All the insects began to cry.

So King Bee became weak and hungry,
And the insects of the kingdom in pain,
So much happiness the flower had brought them
But now the hill looked plain.

One day a cloud was spotted,
It rained on the hills for hours,
And when the rain stopped
The ground just popped,
With one hundred fresh sunflowers.

Now King Bee is happy once more,
And whistling's no longer a chore,
The hill's more hearty,
As the insects throw a party
Much louder and happier than before.

Liam Ramos (8)
Archbishop Sumner Primary School, Lambeth

My Paradise Island

My island is a paradise,
It is nice to escape the winter
And not be as cold as ice,
Everywhere we look the clear blue sky glimmers,
The white sand is so soft it shimmers.

We often wonder for dinner, what will be the dish?
Isn't it obvious?
We are surrounded by delicious fish.
The coconuts fall from the palm trees,
I have not seen palm trees like these
Since my trip to Belize.

One of my favourite activities is chasing crabs,
Be careful that they do not bite you,
Otherwise you will get nasty scabs!
I try to ensure that every day, I go for a swim,
Then as a treat, I look for stones to skim.

The best thing about the island
Is watching the pretty flowers bloom,
They all smell so lovely
And they remind me of my mum's perfume

My island is a paradise,
I wish everywhere was this nice.

Betsy Buckle (8)
Archbishop Sumner Primary School, Lambeth

Jamie The Dragon

J is for Jamie, he was a dragon
A is for Amie, his sister is Amie
M is for me, he likes the word 'me'
I is for igloo, Jamie lives in an igloo
E is for eye, his eye is very small

T is for tiger, they are very dangerous
H is for hyena, they are always surrounding you
E is for elephant, they are very big

D is for dragon, they do breathe out fire
R is for reindeer, they are Santa's helpers
A is for animals, there are lots of them
G is for gazelles, they are a bit fast
O is for octopus, they live underwater
N is for nests, birds have nests.

Sulayman Negash (8)
Archbishop Sumner Primary School, Lambeth

The Magical Candy

The magical candy was magical
And was the best candy of all
It tasted so good and had sweets in it too
It made me feel great like snakes
And I felt greater than ever.
The magical candy gave me another candy
And I ate the first candy and went in Candy World
Once I ate all of them and turned into candy,
I was trying to move but I couldn't move
Boom!
I was back where I belonged
So I got someone to eat the candy
And *boom!* She was in a candy world
And enjoyed it there
But never noticed she was a candy.
Once she did, she got out and they both laughed.

Grace Bayu (7)
Archbishop Sumner Primary School, Lambeth

Do Try, Don't Cry

Do try,
Don't cry,
My mum says to my sister,
When she cries as she struggles to wear her shoes.

Do try,
Don't cry,
My mum says when I cry
That my homework is too hard.

Do try,
Don't cry,
My mum says when I cry
And don't want to read my book.

Do try,
Don't cry,
My mum says when I cry
And don't want to do my chores.

Do try,
Don't cry,

My mum says when you try
You make the work easy,
You learn, practise and have more play time as you complete your work early.
The work becomes fun,
It only happens when you do try and don't cry.

Ayibatonbara Andrew Imgbi (7)
Archbishop Sumner Primary School, Lambeth

The Extraordinary Land Of Candy

Snow-white cotton candy
Gracefully dances in the blue sky
As you enter you know
You've started a brand-new life.

Sun beams down with fiery colours
Making mint grass sprout
And toffee apples grow forever.

Another wonderful day,
Children come out to play,
When swooping, swaying, softly, silently
Soaring in the sky are witches
Coming to invade Candy Land.

Hailstones of rainbow Skittles
Pour down across the land
And witches melt
Into the delicious dark chocolate waterfalls
Warm like lava from a volcano

More extraordinary things await you
In Candy Land.

Chinayah Iyanla Martins-Manuel (8)
Archbishop Sumner Primary School, Lambeth

Music In The Mountains

In a distant land,
On a distant mountain,
In a snow-covered village
Frosted with ice,
The stranger spied children
Chattering by a fountain.

There he stood
By a cone-shaped tree,
In his bony hands
An ivory horn.
In a deep voice he said,
"Now come with me."

The notes began
To flow into the air,
The sound rose up
Louder and louder,
Until it echoed all around,
All the way to his lair.

The curious children
Who now were silent,
Like falling snowflakes,
Followed the sly piper,
As if enchanted,
Who knows where they went?

Constance Palmer (7)

Archbishop Sumner Primary School, Lambeth

Kids' Land

Kids' Land is fun,
It leaves children free to run.
The colours are not dark but light
And shops would give you a free kite,
The buildings are colourful,
There are playgrounds that are wonderful
And children have boosters to take flight.

You share a house with your friend,
Instead of stairs, slides that bend.
I like the swimming pool slides,
And there are lots of fairground rides.
You have your own TV
And a hot tub for free.
There are no schools
And lots of pools.
Adults do shout but kids shoo them out,
What a wonderful world is Kids' Land.

Caroline Monk (8)
Archbishop Sumner Primary School, Lambeth

My Land Is Peaceful

My land is kind
As it is in my mind
My peaceful land is noisy
When I am hurrying
Because they are all scurrying
The flowers bloom
Always as bright as the sun
Even when no one is there
Now my land sounds quite beautiful
But really it can be dangerous
The Basilisk's tooth could kill in a strike
And my imaginary friend could be the end
Most of my animals are quiet, tame and mild
But sometimes they are noisy, lame and wild
So my land is mostly paradise
But never forget it could get nasty and wet.

Edward Goodall (8)
Archbishop Sumner Primary School, Lambeth

Pirate Island

Pirate Island has lots of buried treasure
You will need a map to help you look better
Between the palm trees and park
Count ten places where X marks the spot
Get your shovel and start digging
When you reach the chest
There will be lots of blinging.

Ethan Narvaez (7)
Archbishop Sumner Primary School, Lambeth

Campsite

Campsites are freezing, campsites are cold
I don't want to go camping,
That's what I've been told.
Camping is boring, camping is tight,
My mum said when I get there, I will be alright.
We get in the car, I say, "Bye-bye!"
Dad says, "We're only staying two nights."
We drive off, to the campsite we go.
I wonder what it will be like,
Will there be a rainbow?
We get to the campsite, and I was right,
It's freezing cold and definitely tight.
We set up a fire, and get all cosy.
Soon enough, my cheeks are all rosy.
I guess this might be alright,
I say to Mum who tucks me in.
I say, "I can't wait to stay here another night."

Renée Antonio (9)
Ashburnham Community School, Chelsea

Titanic

A ship called the Queen of Dreams,
Filled with smiles and hopeful beams,
People of Southampton, shouting their goodbyes
Hoping to receive theirs back!
As the Titanic began to say goodbye to them all,
When the seconds waited,
To be well-fated
People shoved, trying to touch,
The floating palace's soft, ocean metal
This day was an extreme memory to remember,
It was 1912, since all of this has happened
But now we are in 2018,
A hundred and six years later, this is still a memory
Of the huge incident.
It is still the greatest ship ever built,
But to me, it's for everyone to remember guilt...

Leemar Alrifai (10)
Ashburnham Community School, Chelsea

Sugar Island

Sugar Island,
The sweetest place on Earth.
Discover the magic of candy,
And get your money's worth.

Where clouds are made from candyfloss,
The sun is a toasted marshmallow.
The ocean's covered in maple syrup,
Floating boats are strawberry jello.

Trees are made of rhubarb,
And filled with sticky toffee.
In the monsoon it pours down rainbow drops,
And the beaches taste like banoffee.

The huts are made of honeycomb
All glazed with cookies and cream,
And the gardens filled with sherbet dips,
It's more than you can dream!

Zayn Merchant Dar (8)
Ashburnham Community School, Chelsea

The Ocean

The sky was blue, the floor was blue,
But all you could see was dolphins,
You'd sit on the beach, watching them dance
And crabs wash up on the shore,
With their little red pincers,
Their bright eyes, you'll never miss them,
Come on now, you can touch it once,
It won't hurt,
Collect shells and build castles,
The beach is a very fun place to be,
You can sit on the beach and play with fun toys,
But the best thing of all, is you having fun.

Moamin Khair (8)
Ashburnham Community School, Chelsea

I'm Not Going To Bed!

I'm not going to bed
Even if my mother told me
I'm not going to bed
Although I could eat some honey!

I'm not going to bed
I don't care
I'm not going to bed
It is not fair!

I'm not going to bed
Even if it is the last thing I do
I'm not going to bed
The person who is, is you!

Iva Shtylla (10)
Ashburnham Community School, Chelsea

Skittles Land

In Skittles Land
King made a band
In his piece of house
Lives a little mouse
Needs to run away
With a quick way
Cows that milk out sweets
There's a caramel tree
That smells like wheat
Come to visit this place
Where you can play with your face.

Ahmed Taha (7)
Ashburnham Community School, Chelsea

Sparkle

M ystical, mysterious and so much more
A lways adventures behind the next door
G iants and goblins have some place to roam
I n a magical place that can be called home
C ome to this party, you'll never be alone.

Leshae Paul (10)
Ashburnham Community School, Chelsea

Friendship

F riendship is always fun,

R ocking hands, side by side,

I love my friends no matter what!

E ast, west, south and north, my friend will be always by my side.

N o fighting, no pushing and no drama happens.

D ay after day, friends we will always be.

S weet as honey, we're gonna be.

H opping and jumping is all we do as friends

I ncredible friends we are

P atient friends can always be fun.

Bibilola Olanubi (8)

Boxgrove Primary School, Abbeywood

Sweet Country

There is a boy called Carr,
And he is in a jar,
He is having a feast,
Although he is the least.

What a wonderful place,
To stuff my face,
Carr is in a land called Lugar,
The place you eat sugar.

There is no brick,
It doesn't need caramel to stick,
The yummy signs are very handy,
I cannot miss candy.

Goodbye Carr,
Lugar, sugar and candy.

Arielle Osayande (7)
Boxgrove Primary School, Abbeywood

Fun World And Boring World

Nutritious World is kind of boring,
But in Candy World it's fun,
Because you can play in the shining sun,
You can play in candy trees
Or you could eat disgusting trees,
You don't need to pay for ice cream,
Or have beans that look like seeds,
Ten out of ten for fun Candy World
And zero out of ten for Nutritious World.

Ngoneh Isha (7)

Boxgrove Primary School, Abbeywood

Sweet Land

Everything is glitter,
It shines in the river.

Some things are small,
Some things are tall.

Things are beautiful,
Things are dull.

But everyone is happy,
No matter what it is like.

Chocolate lanes,
Candy cane lights.

This makes my town so beautiful.

Mya Antwi (8)
Boxgrove Primary School, Abbeywood

Candy Land

In Candy Land
Sugar is the sand!
In the gumball café
They never serve toffee,
Though you can have a chocolate fondue
Then jump on the marshmallows too!

Then you can ride a gummy toad
Up the very rocky road!
Drink from the orange juice fountain
Then climb up the liquorice mountain!

I wish I could live in Candy Land
And not eat food that's canned.

Astrid Davis (11)
Christ Church CE Primary School, Chelsea

Arty-Party

Do you like being arty?
Do you like having parties?
You do?
Well this is the place just for you.

Do you like having bright things?
As well as having light things?
You do?
Well this is the place just for you.

Do you like being artistic?
Go on then, write a poem, an acrostic!

Here, every single sheet
Is very, very, very neat.

The friends you'll see over here,
Are the best friends you'll meet!

Muneera Ahmed (9)
Churchill Gardens Primary School, Westminster

Candy Land

C andy Land, Candy Land
A thing that never should be banned
N ever ever eat too many
D on't just keep on eating any
Y ou might even explode

L oving candy makes you eat loads
A lthough it can make you sick
N ever ever eat it quick
D on't think candy is bad.

Widad Elouassi (10)
Churchill Gardens Primary School, Westminster

Minnie Mouse Land

Welcome to Minnie Mouse Land,
Whenever people come, it should expand.
Look at the silly slide,
When you go on it, you might even glide.
Look at the trampoline, it is such a fantasy,
If you come here, you could conquer your fear,
Come here and you will hear a joyful sound,
It is the best place to be, without a doubt.

Nuha Idris (10)
Churchill Gardens Primary School, Westminster

Candy Land

C an you imagine

A n enormous land

N ever running out of candy

D ealt in your hand

Y ellow, blue, red and pink

C hewing candy will make you think

A bout your lovely colours

N ow you should think about

E ating so many sugary sweets.

Retaj Raed (9)

Churchill Gardens Primary School, Westminster

Sweet Rocky Road

S weet, sweet Rocky Road
W here would I go if you weren't my home?
E veryone in Rocky Road really is tasty
E ven the pillows are made of puff pasty
T ruly, this is the best place to be
S o come on in, and join in with me.

Aishah Wakil (9)

Churchill Gardens Primary School, Westminster

Candyland

Candyland, Candyland, Candyland,
It has sugar sand,
Never, never will your city go,
Sit and watch the candy show,
While you eat your honeycomb,
You may not want to go home,
Go, but not for long,
For there is a candy song.

Sameer Hassan (9)
Churchill Gardens Primary School, Westminster

Luxury Land

Welcome to Luxury Land,
Where everybody's happy.
Mothers don't have to worry,
A baby can change its own nappy,
Books grow on trees,
People eat honey from bees.
Guns are thrown to Mars,
War tanks are turned to cars.
Presents float in the air,
Every little child has a teddy bear.
There is ice cream on chocolate mountains,
Coffee comes out of lakes and fountains,
There are hills of chicken and chips,
People drink juice from rivers in sips.
Deserts of golden sand,
Everybody dreams of this lovely land.

Martey Klu (10)
Dulwich Wood Primary School, Dulwich

Heaven And Hell

Up above the blue, blue sky,
Angels, angels, I can hear them fly,
Singing, dancing, having fun,
Dark angels, hot and flaming,
Dancing in the fiery sun,
The fire raging,
Walls crumbling,
They run around,
Screaming, shouting, screeching, dying,
Still as statues,
Not a single soul moves,
Nobody's having fun,
Everyone's got the blues,
The hourglass turns with a loud, loud noise,
Turning to twelve o'clock, the awkward time,
The hour of madness, the hour of fun,
Walls crumbling with a *bang, bang, bang.*
People dying with a *clang, clang, clang!*
Dancing and singing, having fun,
Shouting, kicking,
Getting badly hurt in the fiery sun,

That's Heaven and Hell,
Now you've learnt!

Nicole Denila

Dulwich Wood Primary School, Dulwich

Sporty Bananas In Pineapple Land

Sporty bananas love having fun,
Sporty bananas jump and they run,
They shoot and they tackle.
Their medical kit keeps them healthy and fit,
In the city where the pineapples live,
The pineapples are foulers,
They're definitely not fit
But the problem with bananas is
That we might split
But we beat them six-one
And most importantly,
We had lots of fun.

Felipe Gomez Seles (9)
Dulwich Wood Primary School, Dulwich

Icelandia Town

In Icelandia Town,
Everything is great.
The happiness never goes down,
Nobody wants to be late!

Snow covers the ground,
Not a speck of green.
As everybody goes around,
It's just a wonderful scene!

Nothing can be more beautiful,
Than the place we call Icelandia,
As everybody slips and slides,
They have a nice time!

Liam Joshua Harvey (10)
Dulwich Wood Primary School, Dulwich

Candy Land

I love Candy Land,
It's bright and grand,
There's a chocolate river,
Where gummy snakes slither
And gummy worms as well
And caramel is gel,
It's where candy canes stand
And there's sugar sand.
It's all so tasty and great
And a bonus is you can stay up late.
Come to Candy Land
And decide your fate.

Joshua Afolayan (10)
Dulwich Wood Primary School, Dulwich

Hogwarts Land

H ogwarts, the magical land

O nly magic in this land

G ryffindor is the best house to have fun

W erewolves are around, so beware or you'll be gone,

A ll the houses are talented and strong

R avenclaw is a clever house, work together, make

T he crowd,

S chool of luck.

Manuela Lo Vecchio (9)

Dulwich Wood Primary School, Dulwich

Wrestling Land

Wrestling, you have fun.
Wrestling, you lose in one, two, three.
Wrestling, you win in one, two, three.
Wrestling, you go to the top rope.
Wrestling, you get flattened by big men.
Wrestling, you get suplexed.
Wrestling is noisy and has theme songs.
Wrestling is cool.

Liam Traynor (9)
Dulwich Wood Primary School, Dulwich

Friends Land

We're like sunflowers
Daisies, meadows
Cherries, daffodils
We are bright fellows!

We dance around
Boys and girls come
To have lots of fun.

And we all know
We'll be friends forever,
We know that
Our land won't end.

Isabella Lola Ali (10)
Dulwich Wood Primary School, Dulwich

The Silly City

In this city,
People are pretty.

A good luck charm
Is nothing to harm.

In the bank
There was a prank.

In the hole
There was a mole.

At the mall,
There was fall.

The hamster
Was a prankster.

Damilola Elizabeth Agbabiaka (9)
Dulwich Wood Primary School, Dulwich

Candy Land

C andy Land is my land
A nd it's the best place to be
N ice, colourful sweets that you can eat
D ancing around in Candy Land is very fun
Y um, yum, yum.

Oluwatamilore Johnson (9)

Dulwich Wood Primary School, Dulwich

The Magical Rainforest

This is a place you might never be,
Imagine it, just for a second
And then you will see
The enormous waterfall
Crashing into the lake,
The water so clear,
You can see water snakes.
Flowers and plants swing every minute,
Over 520,000 rise
Because there is no limit.

The light of the sun drops through the trees,
Down to the shiny, thick grass.
You can identify the living frogs,
Which are made out of glass.

You never know what the weather will be,
All you have to do is wait and see.
Most of the time, it's extremely hot,
Like water being boiled in a pot.
But sometimes it's cooler than usual,
That's no worry, the forest is still beautiful.

The whispers of the wind talk to the animals,
The pitter-patter of the rain helps old trees,
Which are flammable.

The winged lion is being admired by his species
But some of them are so angry and jealous
That they look a bit beastly.
The Octafish glides across the water,
He is even showing off to his daughter.
The squirrel looks cute but scary,
Then he flies across the sky,
He looks like a fairy!

The unicorn, one of the most magical creatures,
Their horn is one of many wonderful features.
This is a place you might never see,
Imagine it, just for a second
And then you will be.

Aileen Ordonez-Castro (11)
Durand Academy, Lambeth

World Of Dreams

Welcome to the World of Dreams,
Where you can be anyone or anything,
Tiptoe like a ballerina
Or fly as if you have wings.

This is the land
Where all your dreams come true.
You can do whatever you want,
It's really up to you.

Sleep on a bed of roses
And a pillow of candyfloss.
Wake up and have sweets for breakfast,
You can become your boss.

In my world,
You can be anything you wish.
You can be a famous celebrity
Or be able to multiply any fraction,
Maybe the fastest athlete
Or just the centre of attention.

This is the land of magic,
Where age has no place.
You can drive when you are five
Or be an astronaut in space.

In this universe,
You can have anything you desire.
It can be a tree that grows real money
Or the greatest invention yet;
A glittery, pink sea.
You could do anything I bet,
You just have to close your eyes and dream.

Cheyanne Meghie (11)
Durand Academy, Lambeth

Teachers

Teachers are everywhere,
In your classroom,
You can never seem to get rid of them!
They see everything that happens,
Teachers, teachers, everywhere.

They are everywhere,
You see them in the halls.
They know where you are,
They know how to fix things,
Always there to help you.

As smart as a computer,
Teachers are always there.
In the lunch hall, everywhere!
They are the ones that teach you everything,
They never let you out of their sight.

They always know what to do,
They're always organised.
If you even try to be bad.
You'll get into trouble no doubt.

Always there to help you along the way,
Teachers just won't go.

Never miss a chance to tell you off,
Teachers are even in the playgrounds.
Teachers are always early,
Teachers are everywhere.
You'll never get away from them!

Chenai Jordan (8)

Durand Academy, Lambeth

The World Of Wizards And Wands

The magic is spreading on Wilbury Island
And is said to soon reach the town Gastrand.
The fight of the wizards is endless,
Yet all those wands appear useless.

As the wind blows those leaves in your face,
The tall waves and the sand start to race.
If you lie down calm on the beach,
You notice the seashells that are out of your reach.

You can feel the power and its strength,
Nobody thinks it's the island or its length.
Everybody knows it's the fight of the wizards
That causes all those terrors and shivers.

The magic is spreading on Wilbury Island,
The waving of wands in the wizards' hands.
There is one world and its glorious bonds,
The world of wizards and wands.

Elena Agostinelli (11)
Durand Academy, Lambeth

The Snow And Grass

The snowy floor beneath my feet,
I wonder how far it goes, a thousand miles deep?
The snow takes me to another world,
A world where my hair is in twists and curls.
It takes me to a place of wonders,
While everybody around me sits and ponders
Where my mind has scurried to.
I laugh in my head, "Silly you!"
I'm just here, standing in the snow,
You really didn't know?

The tall grass beneath my feet stands like spikes,
If you accidentally fall into it, yikes!
If it wasn't for that silly grass,
I'd be able to freely pass.
The snow I like,
So grass, take a hike!

Bethanie Adeyeye (10)
Durand Academy, Lambeth

If You Don't Like Summer

School is out and summer camps start
And older people feel younger at heart
And even at night, it's warm and lazy
If you don't like summer, you must be crazy.

Swim in the pool, eat some ice cream
Stare at the clouds, get lost in a dream
Spin in circles until your brain is hazy
If you don't like summer, you must be crazy.

Go to the beach and build a castle
Or you and your friend in the sand can wrestle
Lie on the green grass, make a chain with a daisy
If you don't like summer, you must be crazy.

Prisca Conteh (9)
Durand Academy, Lambeth

The Old Computer

Entering the dusty room,
Which has never seen a broom,
Wiping the thick dust off the monitor,
Booting up the computer.
Streams of binary on the screen,
Waiting for input...
Loading the game,
Walking around my blocky world,
Where it is grass and stone,
Soon to be flourishing with life.
My digital creation...
Full of life,
People running to and fro,
Minding their own business,
Watching over my creation,
Satisfied at my handiwork,
Then suddenly,
Turning off the computer,
Leaving the room...

Mert Alp Aydin (11)
Durand Academy, Lambeth

Twix Town

Welcome to Twix Town
Where no one ever pulls a frown
The sun's a giant Skittle
The lollipop flowers are ever so little.

Bricks and cement are replaced
With jawbreakers and caramel
And the chocolate rivers made
Of tasty rain that falls off the candy cane trees,
So visit us please.

You can get lots of licks
Of lollipops on their sugar sticks
And get a giant Twix chocolate bar,
Which is far better than gazing
At the stars from afar,
And get a sweet, chocolatey and tasty tour!

Fares Amir Ouanoufi (10)
Durand Academy, Lambeth

New Year Dreams!

I wonder what New Year will be like,
Maybe I'll get a bike.
I bet it will be festive
And the food will be digestive.
Is New Year recommended
Or is it highly prevented?
How long until New Year?
I think it's very near.
Maybe I will play by the sea
And be in the beach ball team.
I hope my family is invited,
I will be so excited.
Maybe we can dance
Or take a trip to France.
New Year is a daydream,
Luckily, we get whipped cream!
New Year come now,
It's today, wow!

Racheal Olaleye (10)
Durand Academy, Lambeth

Imagination

Imagine Land has good, but not bad,
Although they have seven suns
And six hundred moons.
If you come last
You are awarded the first ribbon,
All you have to do is imagine.
Animals that have fifty-one arms
And dogs that bark,
You can teleport to the future
And see Horrid Henry!

In Imagine Land,
You can dream of anything!
Such as, having candy on the road,
Picking your nose and being rich.
There's an Easter Bunny
That pops out marshmallows
And coughs out cream.

Daniel Samuels (8)
Durand Academy, Lambeth

The Lost Puppy

One afternoon in the park,
Chasing after a balloon, I heard a bark.
Something ran in-between my two feet,
Sat on the spot was a cute puppy, biting into meat.
At first, I didn't pay any attention,
A few steps later, I looked in that direction.
To my surprise, when I turned around,
I stood for a while, gazing at what I'd found.
A missing pet from a poster,
It was time to act faster
And break the news to the owner.
That part was not up to a child,
I ran to Dad, who wouldn't mind.

Abigail Daniel Gebresillassie (9)
Durand Academy, Lambeth

Marshmallows On The River

Marshmallows on the river,
All flavours and sizes.
Go to Candy Land,
It will be stuffed with surprises.

Marshmallows are sticky pillows,
They get stuck in my hair.
At least that I can eat them
So I don't really care!

They fly up into the sky,
I pop them in my mouth.
I know they're really high
So each one, I try to count.

I know they're really fluffy,
They're sticky in my mouth.
I jump up high in the sky
And catch them like a butterfly.

Alexia Tianna Clarke (9)
Durand Academy, Lambeth

Chelsea Are The Best

Chelsea are the best,
Other teams are always stressed.
They've won the league five times,
When a game finishes, you hear a chime.

When you go to Chelsea Land,
You always see fans who are banned.
You will hear fans singing,
Even the ones from Beijing.

In Chelsea Land,
You will find nice cars
And they will all be superstars.
Their land is big,
After the match, you can go to a gig.

Come to Chelsea Land
And you'll see all the houses are grand.

Joshua Augustin (11)
Durand Academy, Lambeth

Candy Magic

I love candy magic,
Since it's not tragic.
Candy Magic Land is so sweet,
They also have mouth-watering treats.
There is a jelly mountain
And a chocolate fountain.
That's why you'll see marshmallows bouncing,
But candy magic is not all fun and games,
It can also cause painful pains.
Decay in your teeth
And rot underneath,
Then toothache comes in,
You may feel pain after eating your dinner.
Beware of candy magic
Or else it could end up tragic!

Shyla Dana Fenton-Duhaney (9)
Durand Academy, Lambeth

The Candy City

A boy comes with joy and says...
Knock, knock, knock!
A bag of flour,
A bag of gum,
You can choose,
The trick or treat,
Please leave me
Something sweet to eat.
The boy of joy
Goes into Candy City.
Everything is pretty,
It all tastes strong,
Not a speck of wrong,
One of them is lit,
Caramel makes it stick,
There's a chocolate mousse river,
The gummy snakes can slither,
Come and visit this city,
Where you can be pretty!

Kendra Mauricio Santana (9)
Durand Academy, Lambeth

Pokémon Land

P ikachu is running all around,
O shawott is causing unstoppable chaos,
K angaskhan is stomping around with drought,
É vee won't stop coming in and out,
M ountains shout every day in joy,
O h, what a fun plan,
N o one will ever leave.

L itten sneezes fire everywhere,
A bsol is jumping like crazy,
N othing can stop them together as a team,
D on't annoy them, just kidding!

Andre (9) & Kai Watson
Durand Academy, Lambeth

I Woke Up In The Morning

I woke up in the morning, at quarter to one,
I thought I might have some fun.
I woke up in the morning at quarter to two,
I thought I needed the loo.
I woke up in the morning at quarter to three,
I thought I heard a bumblebee.
I woke up in the morning at quarter to four,
I thought I heard someone at the door.
I woke up in the morning at quarter to five,
I thought I might go for a drive.
And that's the way it is in Sleep City,
Oh Dream City, oh Sleep City.

Dominion Balogun (9)
Durand Academy, Lambeth

The Magic Of Rainbows

Everyone wants happiness, no one wants pain
But you can't make a rainbow without rain.

A rainbow, a rainbow, so many to find,
I wonder what are the different kinds?

There's a rainbow after the rain,
There's happiness after the pain,
So don't give up when life is unfair,
We can stand still and let go of despair.

The rainbow blooms within our eyes,
In ancient promises, there was always excitement.

Rianne Mercurius (9)
Durand Academy, Lambeth

The Mixed-Up Fairy Tale

The dragon and the knight got into a fight
Over the princess in the tower who lost her power.
She wished for a chance to go to the dance,
She had nothing to wear, not a crown for her hair.
She heard a sound so she quickly looked down,
The dragon was slain but the knight was in pain.
She used her hair to lift him up
And gave him a drink from her magic cup.
The knight was healed
But what was that?
He turned into a giant rat!

Izaiah Hudson (9)

Durand Academy, Lambeth

Magic Powers

It all started out with just a few,
For some members,
Their poem I did do.

Imagine their verse by adding a pic,
Finding the right image is the real trick.

Sometimes the search takes a long time
To track one down that's right for the rhyme.

I was encouraged to do a few more,
Little did I know what was in store.

I counted how many I'd done,
The number was two hundred and one!

Christabel Amoah (8)
Durand Academy, Lambeth

4F (My Class)

4F is the best,
4F has success,
Ahmed at the front,
Abu in the middle,
Aznee at the back,
With his pink, big bag.

We walk up the stairs
With our hands on our hips.
If we do that,
There's no school trips.
4F is the best,
4F has success,
4F takes the quest,
But you need to be calm in school,
Especially in the dinner hall.
So don't be fools, just be calm
And be cool.

Ahmed Hagos (8)
Durand Academy, Lambeth

Underwater World!

U nder the water in my land,

N o one will sink or drown.

D ying fish don't exist,

E veryone can swim, not sink.

R eefs as big as football pitches,

W hales are big as boats.

A nchovies slithering around,

T he turtles you mistake for tortoises.

E lectric eels dance to their electrifying sound,

R ace to see my land, it is as fishtastic as it sounds!

Boushra Hagos (10)

Durand Academy, Lambeth

Sweet City

S weets are everywhere, no grass to be seen
W aves of soda are at the beach
E verything is edible, even mud
E very tree is your favourite lolly
T ime is ticking for nightfall

C andy creatures come out to play
I nteresting things can be found
T ime to gather all the treasure you can
Y ou will need them if you wish to build in Sweet City Land.

Ilyaas Gouten (9)

Durand Academy, Lambeth

Magical Place Of Wings

High up in the sky, above the clouds
Let the breeze touch you by
A land of magic all around
Look at the birds in the sky.

We see fairies all so high
Fantastic candy
All so yummy and gorgeous
A beautiful girl called Mandy.

So now you know
All the incredible wonders
All passed by us
Today and in the future
So all the creations and lovers
We say life is beautiful.

Wonuola Amole (9)
Durand Academy, Lambeth

Friendship Land

Friendship is like a golden chain
We have a friendship brain
The flowers have a friendly face
The land has a lovely, delightful space
The land is floating gently anywhere
There is always friendship waiting everywhere
We all dance around, looking for friendship
We wear F-shaped glasses for 'friendly'
But in our land, it goes slowly
Our names start with F, R, I, E, N, D, L and Y.

Samira Tahir Abdu (9)
Durand Academy, Lambeth

Candy Land

Right here in Candy Land,
It is very fun.
You can eat any sweet,
Not all, but some.

It's as good as gold,
Creamy and delicious.
A big space to play,
No one here is vicious.

No terrible trouble,
Not one belly will rumble.
Lots to eat,
Everything is neat.

Lots of rhythm,
The people have wisdom.
It is very grand,
Here in Candy Land.

Shanhi Paris Adelise (9)
Durand Academy, Lambeth

The Weather

The sky is dark and windy,
The clouds are forming quickly.
The sign of rain is coming,
We all go home.

Come, let us play in the rain,
Jump and clap until we drain.
Mum will have the dinner set
And we shall all dine at sunset.

The outside is cold and chilly,
The inside is hot and slippery.
It's time to go to bed,
Until we hear the bird whistling.

Jesse Kobina Afful (8)
Durand Academy, Lambeth

Playful Land

In Playful Land, children play,
Go down slides and enjoy their day.
As fast as cheetahs they run,
Oh, how it is so fun!

Like a dolphin, they jump in the pool,
Like a football player, they kick the ball.
Play with slime,
All the time.

Don't pretend
To make some friends,
If you're bored, play with me,
We can be friends,
I guarantee!

Shakina Mensah (9)
Durand Academy, Lambeth

Renn The Wolf

Renn the wolf, that's me,
Arctic wolf I be.
I run fast through the trees,
No, you'll never catch me!

The forest is my home,
I never feel alone.
I live there with my pack,
They always have my back.

Renn is my name,
No, I don't want fame.
Don't go crazy about me,
I'm just a regular wolf
That lives in the trees.

Harley Taylor (11)
Durand Academy, Lambeth

The Deep Falls Of Snow

The snow is cold,
It's easy to mould.
Quickly, play,
Before it goes away!
The sun is sleeping,
The leaves are weeping,
I'm shivering for a place to stay.

I've got a small ball,
I throw it at the wall.
I think it will stay
But it melts away.
I make an angel
While watching Strange Hill
And slowly, it melts away.

Iqrah Sharifjama (10)
Durand Academy, Lambeth

Candyfloss

C andyfloss is nice,

A s if you're sucking up ice.

N othing is yummier,

D o not waste it.

Y ellow is the best

F or people that wear blue vests.

L ove it so much,

O nly then you will be able to touch.

S o soft,

S weet and yummy in my tummy.

Zerina Turay (10)

Durand Academy, Lambeth

Tropical Island

B eautiful, bright blue sky

A ir as sweet as perfume

R ice and peas, we have to eat

B eaches used for fun and games

A mazing sights for you to see

D elicious foods and tasty drinks

O h my! What a wonderful, awesome place

S inging and dancing to songs by Rihanna.

Myah Lorraine Lewis-Whitley (8)

Durand Academy, Lambeth

Candy Land

C andy Land!

A re you ready for some sweets?

N oses will go red if you eat cupcake trees!

D aily, sweets you can eat.

Y ou get everything for free!

L ots of laughter,

A mazing treats,

N osy doughnuts, beware!

D aily, sweets you can eat.

Fatima Mahfoodh (8)

Durand Academy, Lambeth

Candy Land

Candy Land is a fun place to be
So why don't you come and stuff your face?
If you want to come to Candy Land,
Just jump on the chocolate bar train.
Stuff your face with gumdrops,
Lollipops and Sour Patch Kids,
A very sweet celebration we have in store
So make your next stop be Candy Land for sure!

Tizara Diamond Josephs (8)
Durand Academy, Lambeth

Dragon Country

Welcome to Dragon Country
Where everything looks funny
There are many dragons
Some breathe fire
Others breathe ash
Night Fury is the fastest
Hookfang is the largest
Meatlug is the fattest
And Stormfly is the sharpest.

Welcome to the land of dragons
Where you will get flattened.

Idriis Mohamed (8)

Durand Academy, Lambeth

Doughnut World

Everything is made of doughnuts in my world,
I hear kids clapping their hands to shake sugar off.
I see the creamy custard dripping onto my hand,
I smell the scent of warm strawberry jam.
I touch the soft dough, smothered in sugar,
I taste the deliciousness that lurks inside,
I live in Doughnut World!

Daniel Caldeira Coelho (10)
Durand Academy, Lambeth

Cat In The Hat

Walk and splat in the mud
And land with a thud.
See a giant squid
That squirts a lot of ink.
Float on a boat that will never sink,
Meet the brilliant, skilled cat
Who wears a red and white hat.
Do lots of things with friends every day
And have fun when you play,
So what do you say?

Tristine Wanjiku Kamau (9)
Durand Academy, Lambeth

The Nature

N ight is dark, the stars glisten like diamonds
A pples drop from the trees
T rees sway side to side, dancing with the breeze
U nder the sea, the sea creatures are resting
R ise up with refreshing water from the waterfall
E nergetic animals run up and down.

Kaysha Bailey (8)
Durand Academy, Lambeth

Leaves On The Trees

Leaves rustle on the trees
As they blow in the breeze.
Leaves come in many shades,
Red, orange, yellow and jade.
When leaves fall, I gather them in a bunch
And then I jump in them and hear them crunch.
I think leaves are really pretty,
Leaves are all around my city.

Azario Maigwa (9)
Durand Academy, Lambeth

Vampires

V ampires are really scary.

A wareness, you are really deadly.

M onsters rise from their graves,

P eacocks and ducks are their slaves.

I diotic spiders and centipedes

R un around with cuts and bleed.

E veryone must die!

Nobel Frezghi (9)

Durand Academy, Lambeth

Wolves

W olves howl in the midnight sky
O bey your master or face death
L eave this realm once and for all
V eins in your body will be sucked by my claws
E vening time, say bye to your family
S adness shall be spread across the horizon.

Joshua Frezghi (10)

Durand Academy, Lambeth

My Land Of Sweets

S crumptious, sour sweets

W ith sweets shaped like feet.

E dible, colourful trees and land,

E ven a beach with yummy, sweet sand.

T oday is Sweetie Land's twenty-fifth anniversary

S o come and enjoy some candy!

Nevaeh Boateng (11)

Durand Academy, Lambeth

Christmas Time

I smell tasty turkey and Brussels sprouts,
I hear people singing wonderful Christmas songs,
I see people wrapped up warm,
I taste delicious chocolate bars from Santa,
I touch the Christmas tree as it glows.
Christmas is the best time of the year!

Deborah Daramola (9)

Durand Academy, Lambeth

Christmas Magic

There are happy kids opening presents,
They are always joyful, happy and pleasant.
Children eating chocolates and sweets,
Doing their pleasant meet and greets.
I can see frozen trees and glistening snow
And the Christmas star is starting to glow.

Saron Robel (10)
Durand Academy, Lambeth

Magical Music

I love music,
I love to have fun.
When the sun comes down,
Good times come around.
When music is found,
Don't you frown!
Even when you start to come down,
Just please don't frown,
You'll find a new beginning.

Darryl Asante-Yeboah (11)
Durand Academy, Lambeth

Candy World

S ome places have no sweets
W hen your stomach is upset so
E nter Candy World
E njoy and make your taste buds happy
T ake a few pieces of candyfloss and make
yourself at home.

Fatym Karmoko (9)
Durand Academy, Lambeth

Love Land

It hurts to love someone,
Not to be loved in return.
What is more painful,
Is to love someone
And never find the courage
To let that person know how you feel
And see if they love you back.

Kai Mills (9)

Durand Academy, Lambeth

People

Some people are happy
Some people are calm
Some people are sour
Some people are sad
Some people are skinny
Some people are healthy
Some people are wealthy.

Nathaniel France (8)

Durand Academy, Lambeth

Candy Land

Candy Land has all the candy
You could wish for
But be careful how much you eat!
Enjoy the candy games,
Have as much as you want
And enjoy the candy hotel.

Kareece Stephens (8)

Durand Academy, Lambeth

Notes In The Air

Music is fun,
Music is great,
People use music to celebrate.

Music brings joy,
Music brings laughter,
I can't wait to listen to it after.

Cameron Smith (8)
Durand Academy, Lambeth

Yummy Land

Y ummy Land is delicious,
U ndeniably, it's cool.
M y land is the best,
M y favourite bit is the forest.
Y um, yum!

Micah Licorish (8)

Durand Academy, Lambeth

Candy Court

In Candy Court,
Everything is pretty.
Everyone is nice,
It's not that much of a price.
Everyone is fun,
They do a little run.

Emily Mullen (8)
Durand Academy, Lambeth

Candy Land

In Candy Land there are lots more just like you,
Ask for a sweet in the store,
But there is no caramel crumble
Because it makes your tummy rumble.
There is a chocolate ocean
But you need your chocolate lotion.
Come and visit our place,
Where you can stuff your face.
The sugar rain falls on the floor that's a Flake,
Rainbows appear behind the mountains of cake.
The clouds are blue and pink, it wows me
But it's only the fluffy candy.

Rewan Josef (10)
Holy Cross RC Primary School, Fulham

Monkey Land

In the forest, in a tree,
There's a monkey swinging free,
Hanging by his hands and feet,
Looking for a treat to eat.
Ripe bananas grow nearby,
Soon they've caught the monkey's eye.
Monkey grabs one, starts to peel,
Now he's got a monkey meal!

Shalom Michreteab (9)
Holy Cross RC Primary School, Fulham

Stop Sitting, Get Eating!

I don't mean to be rude
But what do you like for your food?
I like fish and chips
And a diet Coke for sips,
With an ice cream on the side,
As cold as the frozen tide,
So I come and sit at a bare booth or bar,
When a man serves chips and popcorn in a jar,
Then I have a big burger and smack my lips,
Also, some French fries that come with dips.
Time for dessert, the most delicious dessert,
It comes so perfectly, without a speck of dirt.
It's as beautiful as seeing the sunset on a cliff,
It's creamy and smooth, definitely not stiff.
Over it is whipped cream
And a caramel middle, when you bite it, it streams,
So come over here and eat until you go numb,
You can also have dessert and get the last crumb.

Ella Tsang (9)
Hotham Primary School, Putney

This Is... Candy Land!

A wonderful place to go is Candy Land,
Where you suddenly turn into a ginger person
And your house is covered in wonderful delights,
Jujubes, sugar powder and frosting you see,
And bears that are gummy.
Watch out,
They sneak up on you and pounce
To gobble your delicious self up.
Lollipops are the yummy trees,
However, if you climb up,
You'll get stuck!

The river you call the River Thames,
Is not all saltwater, oh no,
It's chocolate milk!
And it's as delicious as ten Oreo milkshakes!
When you enter Candy Land,
You'll see a huge, welcoming banner;
'Welcome to the yummy Candy Land!'
With giant-sized candy canes like elephants!
Well, that's in my opinion,
What about yours?

Directions to Candy Land:
Give a pony/dog candy,
Eat some of yours,
Hug all of your toys,
Do six cartwheels,
Say your favourite dream.
Say your wish for Candy Land,
Finally, you're there!

Don't forget to bring candy
And then the animals will like you there!

Sofia Peon (8)
Hotham Primary School, Putney

Underwater Mayhem

There's rippling sapphire waves,
Dark and beautiful caves,
Gentle, smooth sand,
That's what it's like and,
Coral with as much colour as flowers,
There's no rain here, it never showers,
Seaweed dances to the waves,
It makes you stop, smile and gaze,
That's what it's like in my land,
With a beautiful fish band.

Some fish wear the colours of the rainbow,
Swimming deep down below.
Some swordfish swim like bees,
Through a seaweed patch of tall trees.
A school of dolphins performs elegant loops,
Others swim in circles, in hoops,
While sharks swim greedily looking for prey
But fish are dying, that's not okay.
Now the seas are made of contaminated water,
Killing the fish, father, mother and daughter,
Coral is losing its vibrant colours,

Getting darker and darker
And duller and duller.
We're filling the seas with plastic and hate,
Save this world before it's too late.

Ava Grace McAndie (9)
Hotham Primary School, Putney

Miracle Land!

Once upon a colourful holiday,
While you played, I made this land.
With unicorns that speak,
Chocolate waterfalls and other things,
It is as sweet as a litre of sweets
And full of cats and kittens
And dogs and puppies.
The slides are made of rainbows,
The river is made out of melted chocolate,
The houses are juice boxes
But the best thing is,
The animals fart glitter bombs!

Once upon a colourful holiday,
Kids play with a giant smile on their faces.
When the kids are good,
They get to go lollipop skating
But when a child is naughty,
They have to say, "Sorry!"

All the kids love Christmas,
But most of all, they love music,
It sounds like magic,
The kids all love their lives!

Gemma McLean (8)
Hotham Primary School, Putney

Untitled

Basketball is as fun as Snakes and Ladders
But you need to commit to playing with players.
You have to be a tamed tiger
That's willing to learn,
Players play so well,
People say they're going to burn.

It's very enjoyable,
The best players are unbelievable,
Stephen Curry is as agile as a hamster,
Michael Jordan is a mystical monster.

Basketball players pounce on the orange ball,
The NBA finals are very entertaining
So give your friend a call.
Only two teams can play in the dreaded finals,
People like Kyrie can play in it
Because of their skills.

Samuel Augusto (9)
Hotham Primary School, Putney

Dance Mania

I'd like to tell you about my game
And I'd love to explain the aim.
An exciting, advanced glance
That gives you a chance
To keep you amused and bring happiness.
Now that's the aim, let's talk about the game,
The music will make you kick
And the rhythm will brighten up your day.
It will make you move
And it will make you groove.
You'll get tired and you'll get sweaty
And at the end, you'll look like a happy yeti.
This is my game, I hope you enjoy it,
It's fun and it's different, you will love it!

Matey Grantcharov (9)
Hotham Primary School, Putney

Snow Land

Once there was a pretty place,
Which people could have fun and play.
It was as white as a cloud,
The sparkly snow was causing trouble,
While the children had fun.
The castle in Snow Land, as sparkly as glitter,
The snow-like showers of white.
Snow Land was as cold as ice
But it was not better than the ice stadium.
The sparkly, snowy snow was as soft as a pillow,
It had a special bear to guard the place.
It was the prettiest place on land,
It was as pretty as gold,
Snowflakes dropped onto the land.

Melody Fitzpatrick (9)

Hotham Primary School, Putney

Haunted Horror Land

Haunted Horror Land,
How scary it is.
Everyone is mischievous and gruesome,
Even the youngest kids.

They come out at night,
Give you a fright,
Trust me, over here there is no light in sight,
Everything is dark and nobody cares.

They're here to give you everlasting nightmares,
Running rapidly, I try to escape.
I try to be as fast as Superman
But a bin bag's my cape.

Here I am,
Trying to survive.
Pray for me,
That someone can change my life.

Musa Ahmed (9)
Hotham Primary School, Putney

The Frozen Earth

In this world of my own,
It's adventurous and magical,
There are trees that are as tall as giants.

In this world of my own,
It is tasty
And the trees touch our soft faces.
We can smell the wakening of Earth,
It spreads its fresh scent of mint and lime leaves
From the chocolate tall trees.
When the seasons change, so does Earth,
From frost, icing and bubbly snow,
It hangs on for dear life
But if they fall, they fall gently
To the frozen, frostbitten Earth.

Neva Jansen (9)
Hotham Primary School, Putney

Dream Land

Dream Land is above the clouds,
Where lots of dreams come true.
Ride on anything,
Eat anything you want,
This is Dream Land.

The candy canes are the trees,
Where popcorn grows.
As the wind tickles the candy canes,
The popcorn drops,
It all happens in Dream Land.

You can wish for anything,
Anything you want.
Food, drinks and even wings,
But first, you have to get there,
Before you wish for anything,
This is Dream Land.

Erika Grace Hashimoto (9)
Hotham Primary School, Putney

Fairy Kingdom

In the village of fairies,
Where fairies play,
The fairies don't fly on an aircraft,
But on bees.
They don't have trees like ours,
They have rainbow trees.
They have toadstool houses
And toadstool flats,
The toadstool flats are the best
Because you can see beecrafts.

Friendly fairies play in the playground,
While water fairies swim in the pool.
The fairy pods are like puddles for us,
But fairies think they are big pools.

Annebelle Kruger (8)
Hotham Primary School, Putney

Old Temple

R ight from the entrance, traps will collide

H elp isn't accessible unless

Y ou slide

M ultiplayer game with a good friend

E veryone wins when you reach the end.

C ustom-made characters

R unning through a maze

A vast, old temple made with various blocks of gold

F ires of the ancients, burning long and bright

T reasure chests of gold, lighting up the sky.

Gregory Daniel Hughes (8)

Hotham Primary School, Putney

Uni World

Uni World,
Where you meet a world of magic and fun,
Unicorns play around with their friends,
Like a colourful tribe of fungi.

The houses are so beautiful,
With all their magical music notes.
A rainbow shines so brightly
Upon the candy stalks.

If you look inside a flower,
You'll find all sorts of food.
So come and visit this place
Because it's where you'll find the case.

Alanna Garcia (8)
Hotham Primary School, Putney

The Snow Biome

In my biome,
There is a great snow lion,
He lives in a snow den,
His age is almost ten,
His best friend is a snow hen
And she lives in a snow pen.

They play for long,
They start to play ping-pong,
They sing a loud song
And pretend to be King Kong,
After, they scream and dong.

They go to their house,
As cold as a dead mouse,
The trees are cold
And the bushes are old.

Nnenna Anna Naeche (9)
Hotham Primary School, Putney

Heaven Land

H appiness is everywhere in this place,

E ndless love you will feel.

A ll your dreams will come true,

V ibrant adventures await you.

E verything is wonderful,

N othing bad ever happens.

L ovely memories you will create

A nd keep with you forever.

N umerous friends you will make,

D uring your time in Heaven.

Celo Gilchrist (9)

Hotham Primary School, Putney

Spook Land

Come into the home
Where the psychopaths roam
Where the beasts all roar
And the dragons snore
Spooky sounds
As your heart pounds
Houses open wide
To pull visitors inside
The trees cause pain
As you ride on the ghost train
The whole place is dim
As much as it is grim
The moon is a speck in the sky
If you come, you're sure to die!

Zack River Greenhough (9)
Hotham Primary School, Putney

Food Land

Here in Food Land,
Everyone is happy with two hands.
The land is like a giant plate with giant food,
Everything is tasty, nice and good.
Everyone is made out of types of foods,
But sadly, Mr Orange got lost in the woods.
Everything is yummy, I love it all,
And there is a famous food hall.
I hope you go there and like it,
There, you won't quit.

Bruno Carvalho de Andrade (9)

Hotham Primary School, Putney

Snowmen

S now fills the fields and mountains,
N ot a bit of grass can be seen,
O ver on the white hill, snowmen shout for the royal family.
W hen will they come? Where are they?
M agnificently, they arrive in the snow carriage,
E njoying the freezing breeze, heading for the palace,
N obody is quiet when the palace gates open.

Zoë Sellers (8)
Hotham Primary School, Putney

Dragon Land

D eep beneath the surface of the Earth,

R aging dragons roam this blazing land.

A ngry and dangerous, with fiery breath,

G hastly, gargantuan creatures slumbering slowly across the lifeless landscape.

O nly the bravest of knights would dare to battle these beasts in this

N o-man's-land of menacing monsters.

Haydn Wilkes (9)

Hotham Primary School, Putney

Unicorn Secret Land

In Unicorn Secret Land,
There's a really cool unicorn band.
They sing a famous unicorn song
That doesn't take very long.
Unicorn Secret Land is made of candy
But it can get very sandy.
The sun is always shining bright,
Except for at night.
When the unicorns go to bed,
They have nice dreams in their heads.

Ava Jane Mason (8)
Hotham Primary School, Putney

Candy Land

C olourful candy,

A ll sorts of sweets,

N ot a single piece of fruit,

D on't think people are allowed, they're not,

Y ou will think it's Heaven here.

L ovely places,

A mazing things to see,

N ot a single crisp,

D on't you dare tell!

Sophie Killick (9)

Hotham Primary School, Putney

My Magic Land

M y beautiful land is made of magic,

A s we look around the magical woods, I see Captain Hook looking at me.

G o through the magical way and it will lead you to another day

I n Magic Land, where it rains Skittles.

C an't you just join me on this adventure?

Zoser McCalla (9)
Hotham Primary School, Putney

Cricket Land

C atching is a part of this sport,
R unning slow could cost a wicket.
I nvestigating this sport
C ould give you a thought.
K ettle is boiling, time for tea,
E veryone is so happy.
T ea is in twenty minutes, I should hurry up!

William Saich (8)

Hotham Primary School, Putney

The Sweet World

The land of sweets is joy and peace,
The people are always having a feast.
It always goes right,
The sun is always bright.
The music is soft,
The rocket is off.
The land tastes good,
The chocolate looks like wood.
A magician came,
With his candy cane.

Lina Yoshida (8)
Hotham Primary School, Putney

Candy World

My world is Candy World,
I smell the chocolate coming up to me!
I see that the king is coming
So I need to hide!
I taste the various sweets,
I might taste some I may dislike.
I feel the textures, rough to smooth,
The rough ones will cause some sores!

Shumayl Ahmed
Jessop Primary School, Herne Hill

The Candy World

In Candy City,
Everything's pretty,
No such thing as greens,
You must love King Jellybean,
Cars are made from gummy bears,
If you eat one, do not dare!
The wheels are made from liquorice,
All the sweets are wicked and delish!

Sufyan Ahmed

Jessop Primary School, Herne Hill

What Lurks In The Night Of Minecraft

I love Minecraft but vampires most of all,
Weak ones, strong ones, scariest of them all.

I like Minecraft but I hate zombies,
I love the ice path but not the zombie colleagues.
They like blood and they lurk all night,
They once fell in and they hate daylight.

Some of them are rippers,
They can't stop when they taste blood.
Murderers and snipers
With faces covered in mud.

I like Steve but not as much as the vampires,
The vampires need to feed on someone
Who owns a mundane empire.

Sadaq Asad Ahmed (11)
Jubilee Primary School, Tulse Hill

Munchkin Land

In another land, far away,
Lived some munchkins who went out to play.
There's Popcorn, who always brings some with her,
And Tompkins, who's a bit of a nerd!
Lolly is full of happiness and glee
And Chips is nice to you and me.
Sweetie is a very sweet thing
And in the morning, the birds sing.
Tweet, tweet! They spread their wings
And at that moment, the munchkins sing.
"Gingerbread for houses and candy flowers,
Candyfloss clouds and chocolate towers!"
Fairies dance like twinkling stars
And all day, we eat chocolate bars!
Everything's tasty and everything's sweet,
Every day, we are in for a treat.
"Living in Munchkin Land is a wonderful thing!"
All the little munchkins sing.

Chikamso Ukor-George (10)
St George's Cathedral Catholic Primary School, Southwark

Zombie World And Mine

Block by block, I start to build,
I take every corner of the field.
Not in the day but in the night,
You may see zombies come out to fight.
In my world, it will be frightening,
There will be many strikes of lightning.
You'd better be careful or they'll attack
And try to jump onto your back.
Go into hard mode and you'll see,
They can go in without the key.
There may be destruction
And maybe some abductions.
I know my world like the back of my hand
And will start building, using smooth sand.
Do you want to see my world?
Trust me, it isn't a dreamworld.
I'm trapped in the corner by evil friends,
This is going to be the end,
So goodbye, friend.

Rowlanda Ken-Williams (11)
St George's Cathedral Catholic Primary School, Southwark

Underwater Kingdom

U nder the water

N o one can find you

D ive down to this kingdom

E nter a new world

R each out to the underwater creatures

W ater is clear, you will see the kingdom

A world full of fish and coral

T o the very bottom of the kingdom

E xplore different kinds of plants and coral

R ight next to the place.

K ings and queens all around, come to the palace

I n this palace, there are a lot of things to do

N o one can resist coming here

G o under and live in the kingdom

D own underwater is so cool

O ver the ocean and under the sea

M agical creatures swim under the sea.

Jose Gabriel Abanto (11)

St George's Cathedral Catholic Primary School, Southwark

Candyville

In this land of sugar,
You would not know where to go.
Since there are a lot of places
You really need to know.

In the summer, guess where people go,
They swim in the lake of chocolate milk!
In the winter, guess where people go,
They skate on the blue candy rink.

In this land of sugar, you can eat mud pies
Because they are made of chocolate ganache,
There are frosted cupcake trampolines.

All buildings are made of gingerbread,
The gummy bear statues are so vibrant,
The trees are made of swirly lollipops,
Candyfloss clouds are pink and blue,
There are gumdrop bushes
Where sour cherries grow.

Zarin Anjum Ahmed (9)
St George's Cathedral Catholic Primary School, Southwark

When Snow Comes

Snow and light,
The joy I feel when I see the sky so white.
The joy I feel when I see snow falling
Like a shimmering show!

While icicles crash on the shivering ground,
People smack down Christmas trees with a pound!

I put on my scarf and hat,
To keep me warm like the cat,
As I go out of our flat
Into the snowy path.

It's fun to walk in the powdery snow,
As my boots crunch, ever so slow.
In the whiteness of the snow,
My prints begin to show.

Suddenly, I feel cold and wet,
It's time for me to fret.
Even though I love the snow,
It is time for me to go!

Nathaniel Louis Bernardo Bardos (9)
St George's Cathedral Catholic Primary School, Southwark

Stay At School

School might be cool,
And it will definitely change a fool!
PE is as exhilarating as a roller coaster;
But you'll probably hate lunch,
Make sure to play with your bunch.

You can run, jog and hide,
But I wish we had a slide.
School is bigger than a rhino;
And it's definitely lots of fun
So come in and you'll get a chance to run!

Maybe save up for things,
It might be a cat with a hat!
I'll just say stay at school;
Listen to your greatest teacher
Or else you'll be a big, hairy creature!

Mica-Renee Quiazon (11)
St George's Cathedral Catholic Primary School, Southwark

Candy World

I am always in Candy World,
Never in the real world.
Lollipops and candy canes,
No one is there to make it rain.

Candyfloss and sour sweets
Make me dance to a steady beat.
Every piece of candy I've had
Always makes me the opposite of sad.

There isn't one brick,
Toffee makes it stick.
Unicorns and pretty fairies,
Did I mention that I'm not allergic to dairy?

Rainbows, sunshine, daffodils and daisies,
Don't forget your strawberry laces!

Ivie Channell Ekhibise (10)
St George's Cathedral Catholic Primary School, Southwark

Christmas Wonderland

It's that time of the year
That makes us cheer.
Autumn has broken
And Christmas is open.

Christmas Wonderland is here
And it's time to cheer.
The rides that make us scream
And the ones that make us beam.

Everywhere is festive,
While my dogs are resting.
The rides are a hit
And the guests are in a winter kit.

The smell of eggnog spreads around my world,
It might even spread to the Nether!

Andrea Miles Stallion-Orbista (11)
St George's Cathedral Catholic Primary School, Southwark

Easter Or Opposite

In Easter Wonderland,
Everything is pretty grand.
Flying Easter eggs
With chocolate washing line pegs.
Lick-a-wish rainbows,
Oh yes, white chocolate flows.
Deep in the dark chocolate forest,
Dark chocolate trees attract
All the honeybees.
Chocolate modelling clay,
Makes people shout, "Hooray!"
Sugar-coated birds humming
A mystical song which sends you running.

Rebecca Tenagne Kassa (9)
St George's Cathedral Catholic Primary School, Southwark

Candy Land

Candy Land is cool,
It makes you drool!
It is all yummy,
The animals are gummy.
Friends are here,
Candy Land is near.
Ice is nice,
Not a speck of lice.
Candy Land is fun
For every lovely son.
Flowers are lollipops,
They do have coffee shops.
Bunnies hop,
They don't ever stop!
Come to this land,
Where you can bring your band.

Daryl Gaid (8)
St George's Cathedral Catholic Primary School, Southwark

Candy City

In Candy City,
Everything's pretty,
It all tastes good,
Not an unhappy mood.

There isn't one brick,
Caramel makes it stick.
There's a chocolate fountain
And a toxic mountain.

The trees are still green
But they are filled with ice cream.
Come and visit this place,
Where you can stuff your face.

Alicia Oyedele (11)
St George's Cathedral Catholic Primary School, Southwark

Candy Land

I love candy,
It's so yummy.
It makes my tummy
Really funny.

You can eat the trees,
You can also eat the leaves.
Come to Candy Land,
Where you feel grand.

Even if it's raining or sunny,
It always makes me happy.
It's the best place to be,
Come and see!

Vernice Cuevas (8)
St George's Cathedral Catholic Primary School, Southwark

A Secret Garden

Everything's perfect
Roses don't die
Scented flowers
Forever they thrive.

Orchids dance
To the morning breeze
Marigolds sing
With the birds and the bees.

Whistle of the leaves
Song of the air
Love of the sunflowers
Happiness is everywhere.

Julianna Ysabelle Valenzona (11)
St George's Cathedral Catholic Primary School, Southwark

Imaginary Land

I magine if you will, a

M agical land, where no one has been before.

A mazing stars shine brightly all around,

G lowing balls of light change colours in the sky.

I magine living in such a land!

N ine million people live here,

A nimals are friendly, clever and cute.

R ainbows here have twenty different colours,

Y ou will be amazed at what you see here!

L ots of trees produce amazing fruit

A nd yummy food makes you want to eat more.

N o one is sad or bored in this place,

D reams come true!

Nathaniel Marfo (10)
St John The Divine CE Primary School, Camberwell

Candy City

Candy City
Is a land of delicious fun,
With lots of children stuffing their mouths.
The sucking sounds and the bubblegum pops,
The popping candy sounds so good.
People think it might end so soon
But that is so not true.

Candy City
Is fun like Thorpe Park.
You can do whatever you like,
Come whenever you like
Because it's never too late,
You even have a house in the mist of candy!
Just know that there will never be
An end to Candy City!

Camilla Kai Mensah (10)
St John The Divine CE Primary School, Camberwell

Computer Land

A land where anything goes,
Giant, epic ducks fly
And frogs have ten toes.

A land where
UFOs shoot across the sky
And clouds rain M&Ms,
That pile mountains high!

A land where robots befriend fluffy bunnies
And Pac-Man fights Mario
Over a pot of honey.

I would like to live in Computer Land,
A land where everything goes.
I would play night and day
And there forever, I would stay.

David Alejandro Hannam Valles (9)
St John The Divine CE Primary School, Camberwell

Nightmare Land

Beware! Be warned!
A spooky place,
Armless zombies
All over the place.
The moon is cracked,
The rain is made of juicy blood,
There's no way out!
So everyone come in,
Never to live in this spooky place.
Keep walking, keep walking,
You see a big place.
Armless zombies all over the place,
It never stops raining juicy blood.
Come and get your poisonous sweets,
Come and get your free zombie pets!

Inayaht Hussain
St John The Divine CE Primary School, Camberwell

Fun Land

In Fun Land,
You will find;
Children laughing loudly,
Fairies dancing delightfully
And singing animals.

In Fun Land,
You will find;
Bread, candy, oranges,
Board games and the Fun Queen!

In Fun Land,
You will find;
Marvellous bread,
Oranges that taste like milk
And sweets that taste like Haribo.

In Fun Land,
It's so fun,
So come for free!

Andrea Carrera (9)
St John The Divine CE Primary School, Camberwell

Vegetable Land: Where All Are Welcome

V ery vegan
E lements of health
G oing into the forest to get some fruit
E ven adults come here
T astes buds go over the moon
A lso, we're as cool as cucumbers
B lasting with flavour
L et your child come
E veryone is welcome.

Rihann Mitchell
St John The Divine CE Primary School, Camberwell

The Halloween Nightmare Land

You have arrived at your destination,
You see a forest,
You see a path,
Come here, you may never last.

You have five hours,
According to time,
Don't kill,
You'll die.

You will never leave,
You may always die,
Come here, see what's behind.

Maya Abdelwasi
St John The Divine CE Primary School, Camberwell

The Arctic

A n endless desert of white, miles of nothing.

R ain, frozen and damp, building a mountain.

C old water with waves as big as waterfalls.

T iger, white far and near surviving here in the wild.

 I ce, dangerous and freezing, slippery and wet.

C old, it kills many lives and never stops, never.

Lara Talbot (10)

The Chelsea Group Of Children, Wandsworth

Rainbow Village

An amusing place
Where there's lots of space.
It's a picturesque land
With coloured sand.
There's a part that is scary
But the rest is glary.

Gabi Reder (10)
The Chelsea Group Of Children, Wandsworth

YOUNG WRITERS INFORMATION

We hope you have enjoyed reading this book – and that you will continue to in the coming years.

If you're a young writer who enjoys reading and creative writing, or the parent of an enthusiastic poet or story writer, do visit our website **www.youngwriters.co.uk**. Here you will find free competitions, workshops and games, as well as recommended reads, a poetry glossary and our blog.

If you would like to order further copies of this book, or any of our other titles, then please give us a call or visit **www.youngwriters.co.uk**.

Young Writers
Remus House
Coltsfoot Drive
Peterborough
PE2 9BF
(01733) 890066
info@youngwriters.co.uk